THE PREPPY CAT

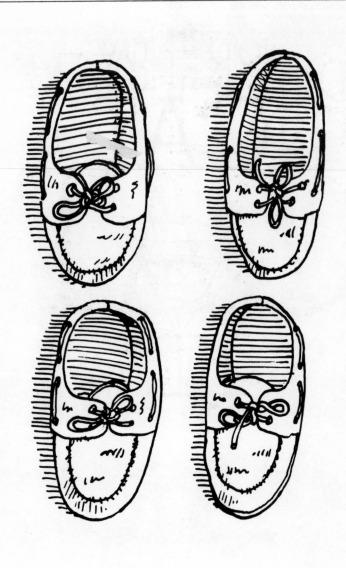

THE PREPPY CAT

by J. C. Suarès,
Jeff Weiss and Dan Weiss

BERKLEY BOOKS, NEW YORK

THE PREPPY CAT™

A Berkley Book/ published by arrange-
ment with Cloverdale Press, Inc.

PRINTING HISTORY
Berkley trade paperback edition/April
1982

ISBN: 0-425-05724-0

**PRINTED IN THE UNITED STATES OF
AMERICA**

*The authors acknowledge the superb
assistance of Alfred Gingold and Marion
Mundy, and Sandra Berg and the Grand
Hotel Olafson.*

CONTENTS

AN INTRODUCTION

AN INTERVIEW WITH ORIANA FELINACCI AND LELAND STANFORD CAT XVII, THE PREPPY CAT

OF: So, Mr. Stanford. You are the famous preppy cat.

PC: Indeed!

OF: Mr. Cat, all over the world cats are starving. In New York, Paris, Istanbul, millions of cats are homeless, ill, uneducated.

PC: I know. Icky, isn't it?

OF: We may be on our way to the endangered species list. Yet you've written a book that many regard as a relic of a bygone era: a book full of how to behave at the country club, what to wear to a party, what to say on a date. How can you?

PC: It's a dirty job, Ori, but somebody's got to do it. Someone's got to educate these poor kittens or they'll never get anywhere. Besides, you think I have it easy? Say, would you like a little drinky? I get so *thirsty* when I talk politics.

OF: No thank you. You were saying?

PC: (Drinking) Mmmmmmm, love that cream. Where was I? Ah—well, things are tough all over, that's all. Club dues, gas for the Mercedes, the tailor. Do you know you have to special-order fresh mice at the butcher nowadays? They only stock frozen!

OF: But surely you don't think that your problems—

PC: I'm setting an *example*, Ori. Someone's got to show those less fortunate they can rise above their litter in life.

FAMILY TREE

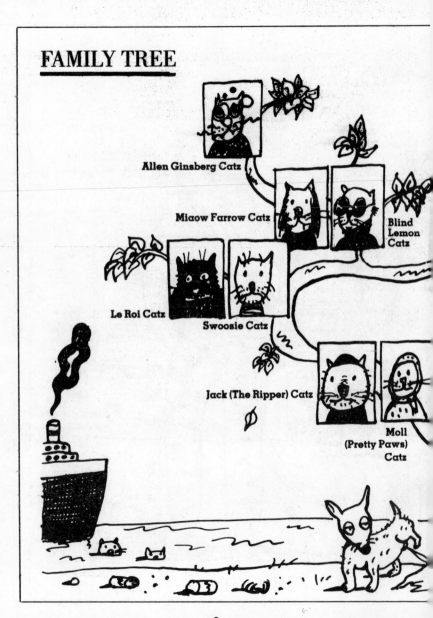

Allen Ginsberg Catz

Miaow Farrow Catz

Blind Lemon Catz

Le Roi Catz

Swoosie Catz

Jack (The Ripper) Catz

Moll (Pretty Paws) Catz

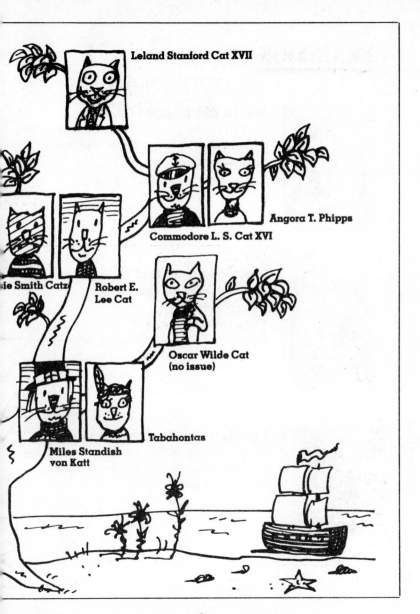

Leland Stanford Cat XVII

Commodore L. S. Cat XVI

Angora T. Phipps

sie Smith Catz

Robert E. Lee Cat

Oscar Wilde Cat (no issue)

Miles Standish von Katt

Tabahontas

YEARBOOK

Morris: Most likely to succeed
"And with residuals and spinoff endorsements I'll need all the tax shelters I can get, so let's see ..."
Jazz Club V–VI

Leo: Gone Hollywood
"So who cares if I don't get billing. Where's Lassie now?"
Film Club IV, V, pres. VI

Felix the Cat: Mr. Entertainment
"And then we let all those mice loose on the dance floor, see? Laugh? I thought I'd pop my collar."
Comedy Club pres. IV–VI

Fritz the Cat: Class Freak

*"So, like then, we really—what? Oh, wow, I mean
that really does it, you know?
Hmmm? Oh, wow."
Yoga Club IV–V, NORML campus founder and
pres. V–VI*

The Pink Panther: Homecoming Queen

*"Of course it's my natural color!"
Judy Garland Fan Club pres. III–VI*

Leland Stanford Cat XVII

*"It's how you play the game."
Tennis I–VIII, Stones and Bones II, Angling V*

SOCIAL REGISTER

Leland Stanford Cat XVII, the first cat ever admitted to the Maidstone Club. His mother, Angora T. Phipps, owns the finest collection of pre-Raphaelite litter pans on the East Coast (collection on display at Mewseum of Modern Art). His great-uncle, Henry "Tiger" Baum, charged up San Juan Hill disguised as Theodore Roosevelt's muffler. Leland's sister, Susie "Lion Eyes" Stanford, made her debut at Le Grande Cotillion des Petites Chattes in Watermill in 1979. A subsequent arrest for catnip in the dorms at Sweetcream Junior College did little to dampen this enthusiastic socialite, and she and her brother are fixtures at feline festivities from Palm Beach to Bar Harbor.

THE KITTY LEAGUE COOK BOOK

PETITS FRISQUIS AU NATUREL

Ingredients: One bag of dry nibbles.

Method: Locate bag wherever it is stored. Place yourself in close proximity to same. Raise paw. Extend claws. Using downward motion, create opening in bag. If bigger opening is desired, use teeth also. Consume pellets as they fall, or, if you prefer, wait until sufficient quantity has accumulated on floor before dining. Recipe may be doubled, tripled, quadrupled, quintupled, sextupled, septupled.

CREAM OF CREAM AND TUNA CATSEROLE

Ingredients: One can cream of cream soup.

One can tuna fish.

Method: Jump up on kitchen counter. Knock one open cream soup onto floor. Lick up half cup, reserving remaining one and a half cups for decoration. Pad carefully through and around remaining cream, making decorative pattern on floor. Immediately leave kitchen. Sit on bookcase until cream has been removed from floor. Lick cream off paws. Return to kitchen. Meow loudly. Open tuna can, consume contents. Serves one.

GROUND MEAT PATTIES (For Tailgate picnic)

Ingredients: Four meat patties.

Method: Push meat patties off tailgate onto ground. Serves four.

MINUTE MICE (Serve in Baccarat bowl)

Ingredients: One or more medium-size field mice or meadow voles.

(Note: Brown mice are higher in Vitamin B. White mice, though tasty, are somewhat harder to obtain, but well worth the effort of hanging around a laboratory. Bar Harbor, Maine, a key vacation spot, has a super lab.)

Method: For each serving, quickly stalk one small-to-medium mouse until done in. Drop mouse on step at back door of house. Walk away. If company is expected, leave mouse at front door as sign of welcome.

FRIED FROG FROID (Excellent for vacation on Nantucket)

Ingredients: One frog per serving.

Method: Proceed as above, substituting frog for mouse. Gently sauté frog on low heat. Allow to cool. Whoever discovers this dish will be thoroughly chilled, especially after a bad night.

TRADITIONAL PLACE SETTING

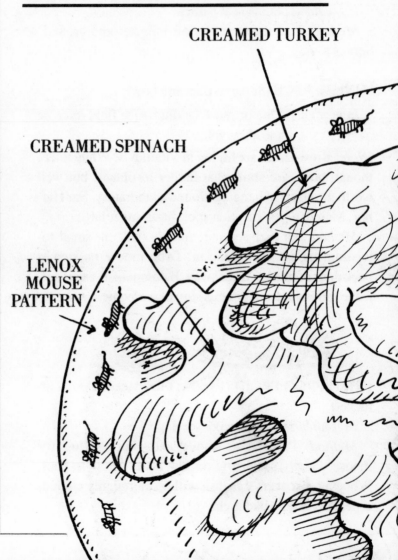

CREAMED TURKEY

CREAMED SPINACH

LENOX
MOUSE
PATTERN

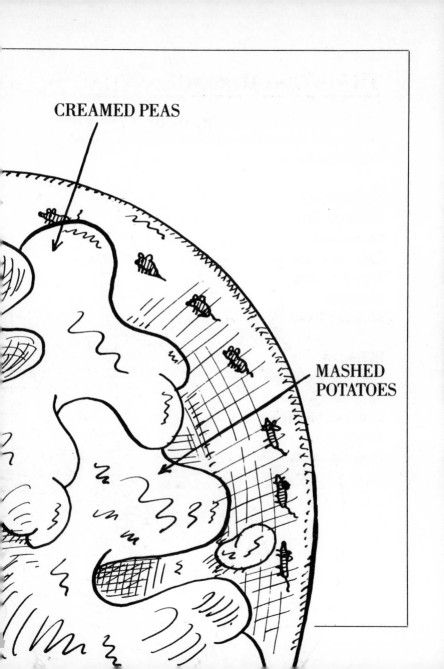

LIBATIONS

It's utterly important to know the right drinks to serve your guests. Kit and Pawsie tell us these are outstanding at cattail parties.

Mixed Drinks
Whiskers Sour
Meowgarita
Cata Tonic (that's how you get after a few of these)
Tomcat Collins
Mancattan
Milk and Tonic

Wines
Cateauneuf du Pape
Purrgundy
Catbernet Sauvignon
Pouilly Pussé
Dom Purrignon

MOUSETINI

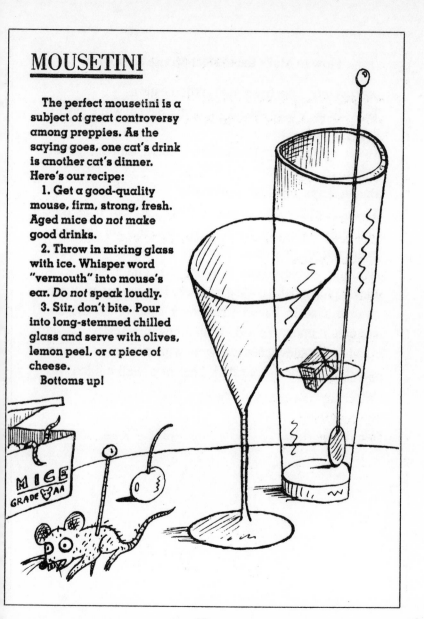

The perfect mousetini is a subject of great controversy among preppies. As the saying goes, one cat's drink is another cat's dinner. Here's our recipe:

1. Get a good-quality mouse, firm, strong, fresh. Aged mice do *not* make good drinks.

2. Throw in mixing glass with ice. Whisper word "vermouth" into mouse's ear. *Do not* speak loudly.

3. Stir, don't bite. Pour into long-stemmed chilled glass and serve with olives, lemon peel, or a piece of cheese.

Bottoms up!

MICE
GRADE AA

How to Make the Perfect Mouse Sandwich

Ingredients: One fresh mouse (domestic).

Two slices whole wheat or home-baked white bread, thinly sliced, sans crust.

Sweet butter or mayonnaise, iceberg lettuce, pickle chips.

Bacon strips, cheddar (optional).

Method: Make sure mouse is freshly killed. If its nose and eyes shine, it's fresh. If it stays still for freshness examination, it's dead. Remove tail. Place on slice of white or whole wheat. Mayonnaise, butter, lettuce, or pickle chips make good garnishes. For variety, try wrapping mouse in bacon strips or a slice of cheese and running it under the broiler for a few minutes.

Mouse sandwiches go well with potato or spinach salad. To drink, serve dark beer or a well-chilled Moselle.

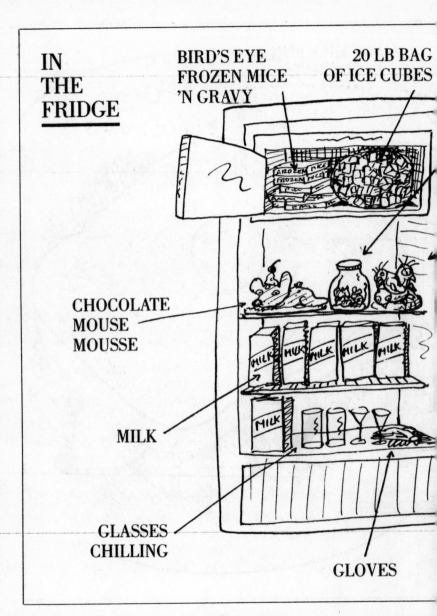

IN THE FRIDGE

BIRD'S EYE FROZEN MICE 'N GRAVY

20 LB BAG OF ICE CUBES

CHOCOLATE MOUSE MOUSSE

MILK

GLASSES CHILLING

GLOVES

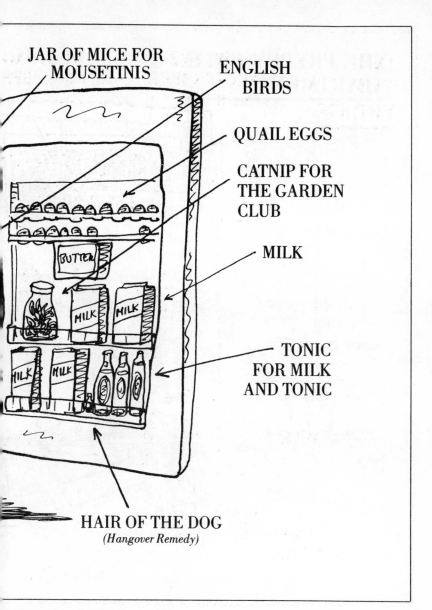

JAR OF MICE FOR
MOUSETINIS

ENGLISH
BIRDS

QUAIL EGGS

CATNIP FOR
THE GARDEN
CLUB

MILK

TONIC
FOR MILK
AND TONIC

HAIR OF THE DOG
(Hangover Remedy)

THE PREPPY CAT'S APARTMENT

Good taste is timeless, so nothing changes in the world of preppy furnishings. An occasional dusting is all these venerable digs need to be forever, as they say, swell!

1. Duck lamp.
2. Currier and Ives print depicting cats riding to hounds and back again.
3. Well-worn horsehair sofa is soft enough for sleeping, nubby enough for scratching, and nonallergenic for sensitive felines. (An afghan throw makes a nice touch.)
4. Curtains were last closed for Halloween party in 1969. Bunched and laddered, they are an easy stairway to sill.
5. Well-stocked bookcase, containing *The Annotated Puss in Boots, The World According to Garfield, The Feline Mystique,* and others (see Fave Reading List).

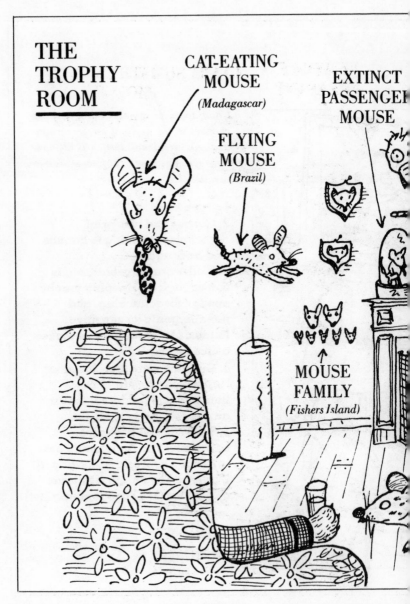

THE
TROPHY
ROOM

CAT-EATING
MOUSE
(Madagascar)

FLYING
MOUSE
(Brazil)

EXTINCT
PASSENGE[
MOUSE

MOUSE
FAMILY
(Fishers Island)

NEWPORT PHEASANT

GIANT SUMATRAN MOUSE

NANTUCKET MOUSE

GIANT SPOTTED MOUSE
(Africa)

BROWN MOUSE
(Palm Beach)

27

THE WELL-DRESSED PREPPY CAT

Class ring is acceptable on cats out of college fewer than five years. Cats who've gone to wrong school needn't bother.

Necktie is nice touch for formal occasions (weddings, conventions, balls). Be careful tie doesn't clash with fur and that it covers flea collar. A loosely tied tie is worse than no tie at all. Ascots are always vulgar.

Lamouse shirts: Great for casual wear. Come in 9,287 colors. Get them all. Never worn with top hat.

Argyle socks: Useful for potato-sack racing, chewing, hiding catnip stash. Preppy mothers advise buying in fives in case of hole or loss.

DOWN VEST KIT

Instructions for Assembly

1. Secure vest kit on nonabsorbent surface.
2. Kill kit, making sure feathers are clean.
3. Pluck kit; remainder is delicious roasted with chestnut stuffing.
4. Sew feathers into vest; wear with plaid shirt, chinos, and loafers.
Talk about hunting a lot. Alternately, discard vest and go back to
eating the kit.

THE GREAT OUTDOORS

FISHING KIT

SIERRA CLUB TAILPACK

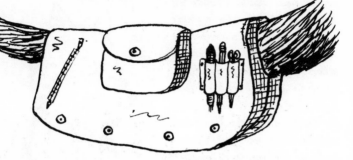

SWISS TREE-CLIMBING TOOL

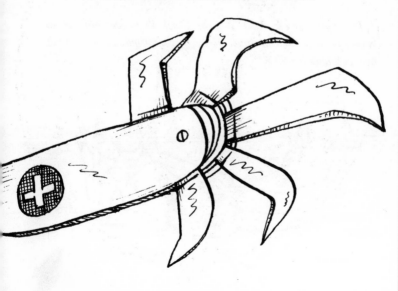

1. Our extensive selection of webbed flea collars. Casual yet distinctive. Order yours in choice of school stripes, club crest, or design of tiny whales, lobsters, or other seafood. Water-repellent. Sterling silver buckle reflects light after dark. Allow six weeks for monogramming. Also available in kitten size. 100% cotton version for warmer weather. Stripes and solids only.

2. Don't go near the water. But she'll look oh-so-charming in our boyleg swimsuit by Catalina. Discreetly covers spaying scars. Only her vet knows for sure.

3. For the cat who has everything, a sterling silver flea-powder canister with shaker top. Away with that unsightly can on the dresser. Monogram or name up to 39 letters.

4. Imported delicacies. Treat Tabby's and Tom's tummies to these yummies. Cream of Canary Soup, Duck Soup, Trout Chowder, Woodchuck Liver Pâté, Smoked Mouse Ears, Mediterranean Ratatooey.

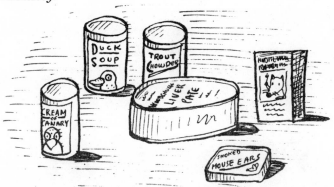

5. We know how you hate wet feet. Stay dry and fashionable in our leather and rubber casuals. Pink, green, pink and green, or green and pink. Sets of four.

DISTINCTIVE DINING

1. Royal Doulton bone china dish with family crest. Hand-decorated. Coordinated stemmed water goblet. Will not tip over.

2. Place mats. Charming design of ducks and cattails. With choice of monogram or name in script. Nonspill rim. Gold border. Waterproof.

THE CAT AT HOME

1. Relax in fashionable comfort. Comfy wicker single bed with madras mattress. White or natural. Stunning in garden room or conservatory.

2. Covered litter box in traditional khaki with maroon or blue stripe. Or special-order the box in school colors with crest. High-impact styrene.

3. Unique convertible slipcover. Starts out as a traditional floral-print 100% cotton chintz cover for English-style wing chair. You can convert the fabric to nubby tweed all by yourself. Hours of fun.
4. When you want to be alone. Spend your leisure hours in the privacy you deserve. The ultimate in understated elegance — our simple corrugated brown box. With optional plaid liner. Also available in easily collapsible lightweight form.

GREAT GIFTS

1. *Enter in elegance. Your very own traditional entrance door. Comes with brass name plaque and your own door knocker, a tiny brass lion head, just like No. 10 Downing Street.*

2. *Herb garden planned just for you. Comes with five packets of seeds and instructions for digging.*

3. *Charming cachepot. Limoges cachepot for a bunch of catnip or catnip houseplant. Or an elegant home for a cattleya orchid.*

4. *Have summer all year round. Super sandbox. Keep the memories of your vacation. Just like the ones on the Cape. Green wooden frame. Comes with shovel and pail. Four side seats for perching. Kitten-size version too.*

OUR JUNIOR SECTION

1. And don't forget the kittens. Our fine selection of timeless toys and accessories. Mousieland: Favorite game of the younger set. Similar to Parcheesi. Tons of fun. Includes four mice, four cheese wedges, four kittens. Ages 6 weeks to 6 months.

2. Never too young for the classics. Madras catnip mouse with jingle bell inside.

3. 100% wool Irish heather yarn balls to unravel. Muted tones. Develops coordination.

4. Birdie mobile. Hand-carved in Vermont. For your scratching post.
Features ducks and garden species. Get to know the birds early! Also available with goldfish and guppies.

5. Important Claws. Your youngster will learn to scratch with our favorite tweed Santa Claws. Stuffed with 100% Chinese goose down. Guaranteed to leak.

6. For calico kittens. Charming calico pinafore by Florence Eisecat. One size fits all.

7. Pink and green, navy and green purrsonalized T-shirt, also by Florence Eisecat.

8. The all-time classics. Set of three pop-up books: Puss in Weejuns, Grimm's Fairy Tails, Three Blond Mice.

9. Just like Mummy and Daddy! Mini-furniture set with tiny slipcovers to demolish. Traditional style with crewel pattern. Set includes couch, easy chair, and ottoman.

10. Ivy league friends. Lovable pillows to snooze on. Choice of Boola Boola Bulldog or Prince Tony Tiger. Imported from Germany.

ATTACHÉ CASE

YARN

SNACK

L.S.C. XVII

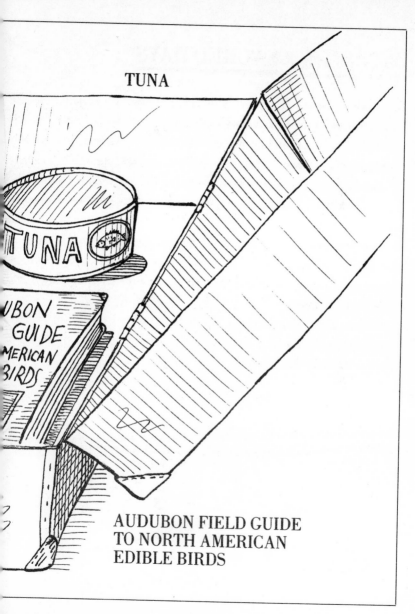

TUNA

TUNA

UBON
GUIDE
MERICAN
BIRDS

AUDUBON FIELD GUIDE
TO NORTH AMERICAN
EDIBLE BIRDS

SACRED DAYS

1. Sandy Dennis's Birthday: This selfless creature runs a hotel for fallen felines. Cares for twenty-eight cats. Won Nobel Peace Furball in 1978. Each year on her birthday thousands of raucous preppy cats convene on her lawn for peace, napping, and mating.

2. Any Al Stewart concert: Don't miss his live version of "Year of the Cat." He adds censored verses; purring on the choruses is encouraged.

3. Independence Day: Preppies celebrate this traditional holiday in the traditional way, by urinating along the borders of their homes. Nonpreppies seem to understand and respect this observance and keep their distance.

4. Kliban Day: The preppy's Mardi Gras. Cats wear funny outfits, sing funny songs, play with funny spinoff products, sit down to traditional meat-loaf dinner.

SAMPLE INVITATION

Mr. and Mrs. Felix T. Cat take pleasure in inviting
you to the wedding of their daughter
Anastasia
to the son of Mr. and Mrs. Cat Mandu
Jerry
in the Angora Lounge of the Kitkat Club
Cream and catnip will be served
Flea collar optional

R.S.V.P.

45

HOW TO PICK UP FEMALES IN A BAR

1. Establish eye contact.
2. Purr provocatively.
3. Sip drink (optional).
4. When you're sure you've got her undivided attention, subtly fli[ng] self across bar, landing on female. Gouge, maul, bite, kick, scratc[h] chew affectionately. Try not to draw blood.
5. We'd describe this step in full, but it's gross.
6. The rest is silence. Ask her what she's thinking.

HOW TO PICK UP FEMALES IN A BARN.

1. Establish eye contact.
2. Purr provocatively.
3. Chew straw (optional).
4. When you're sure you've got her undivided attention, subtly fling self across barn, landing on female. Gouge, maul, bite, kick, scratch, chew affectionately. Try not to draw blood.
5. We'd describe this step in full, but it's gross.
6. The rest is silence. Ask her what she's thinking.

ALLERGIES

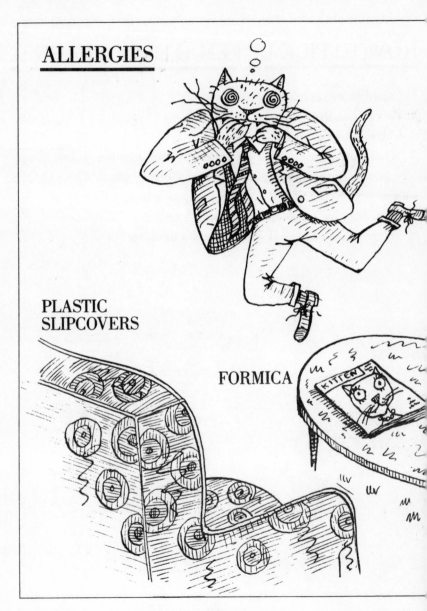

PLASTIC SLIPCOVERS

FORMICA

KITTEN

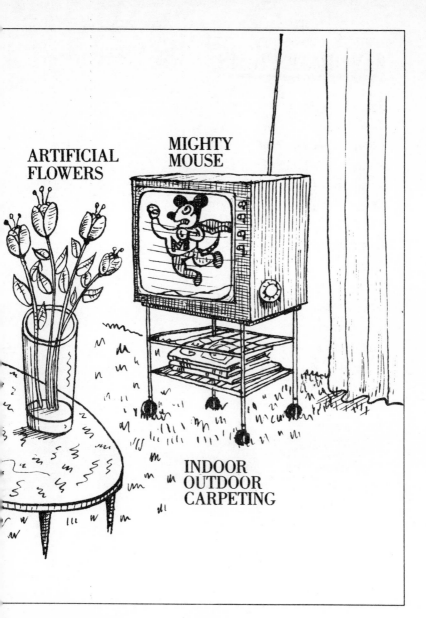

ARTIFICIAL
FLOWERS

MIGHTY
MOUSE

INDOOR
OUTDOOR
CARPETING

FAVORITE FILMS

Save the Tiger
Torn Curtain
Cat on a Hot Tin Roof
Paws
A Nap in the Sun
Ordinary Felines
The Pride and the Persian
Last Tuna in Paris
Stripes
The Yowling
Duck Soup
The Mousetrap
The Black Cat
Top Cat
Tiger Bay
Any *Pink Panther* movie
The Leopard
The Cat People
Cat Ballou
Harry and Tonto

51

PREPPY CAT FAVE READING LIST

T.S. Eliot's *Old Possum's Book of Practical Cats*
The Scarlet Litter
The Cathouse at Pooh Corner
Purrcy B. Shelley's Collected Poems
Tomcat Sawyer
Mewsweek
The Shoes of the Fisherman
A Tail of Two Cities

Of Mice and Manx
The Mouse of Seven Gables
The Thorn Birds
The Three Mouseketeers

THE WELL-READ CAT

A preppy cat is a literate cat. No one wants a cat around who wouldn't know Proust from Pritikin. Still, life is short, even if you have nine of them. Boating, tennis, travel, the club scene—all these and more cut into the reading time of all but the most studious cats. This list is designed for the cat who needs to sound well-read without actually reading. Simply memorize the quotes and you'll be ready for anything.

Mother was put to sleep today. Or perhaps yesterday. I'm not sure.

The Strange Cat, *Albert Camew*

Padding up alongside the coal hod, Camilla felt the fur on the back of her paws crackle, the fine hairs tickling the thickened, inflamed flesh in which were imbedded her knuckles.

Lady Catterley's Lover, *D.H. Lawrence*

If you really want to hear about it, the first thing you'll probably want to know is where I was littered, and what my lousy kittenhood was like, and how my parents were *catatonic* and all because they had me and all that Dickensian crap but to tell you the truth, that stuff bores me and besides, I think it's catty.

The Cat-cher in the Rye, *J.D. Salinger*

So we beat on, paws against the current, borne back ceaselessly into the past.

The Great Catsby, *F. Scat Fitzgerald*

It was sunset on Sunset. I checked myself in a nearby puddle before scratching at the door. My fur was clean, my collar snug, my claws trimmed. I looked like quite a cat, all things considered. I had to. I was calling on six million dollars' worth of liver bits in cream sauce futures and I was asking for a job.

Farewell, My Persian, *Raymond Chandler*

We had mountains on the Missouri shore and heavy timber, fine for scratching on the Illinois side. We laid there in the sun all day and watched the rafts and steamboats spin down the Missouri shore and then we caught and et some fish. Jim wanted to go for birds. But, no I said, 'twasn't half safe. Sometime later a dog came by trying to sniff out old Jim. But we climbed a tree way up high. Widow-woman had to come fetch us down.

Huckleberry Paw, *Mark Twain*

Call me a small male.

Moby Kitten, *Purrman Melville*

Why are we by all creatures waited on?
Why do the prodigal elements supply
Life and food to me, being more pure than I?

"Holy Sonnets," *John Donne*

Thus sang the uncouth swain to th' oaks and rills
He touched the tender buds of catnip hills
Arose to greet the sun with fur so grey
That mighty heavens hailed his tail this day.

"Lycidas," *John Milton*

But the object that most drew my attention . . . was a certain affair of fine
red cloth, much worn and faded. There were traces about it of old
embroidery, which, however, was greatly frayed and defaced; so that none
or very little of the glitter was left. There were faint traces of leather strap
and buckle to where it had once been joined to the collar of its owner,
indeed the faint aroma of a poultice to ward off fleas still clung to it. This
rag of scarlet cloth, on careful examination, assumed the shape of a letter.
It was the capital letter "L".

The Scarlet Litter, *Nathaniel Pawthorne*

The fog, and me, come in on little cat's feet.

"Fog," *Carl Sandburg*

Thou wast not born for death, immortal bird!
No hungry generations tread thee down
The voice I hear this passing night was heard
By felines in an ancient Pharaoh's town.

"Ode to a Nightingale," *John Keats*

HUNTING

MARINE BIOLOGY

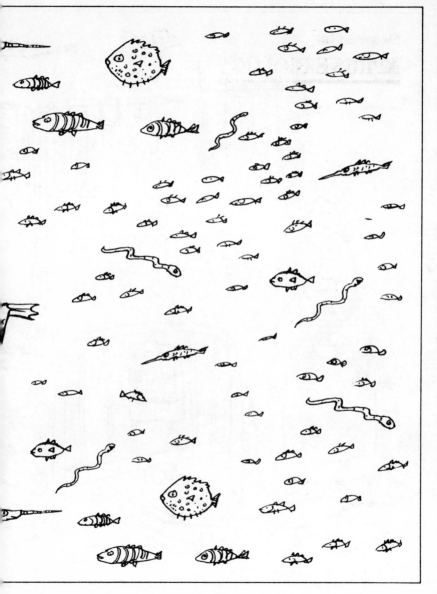

APRÈS SKI

THE NIGHTMARE

GENTLECAT'S AGREEMENT

You discover your sister is dating a mutt. Not just a dog, though Lord knows that would be bad enough. I mean a mutt, a mongrel, a beast of unknown parentage!

It's no joke. Lives have collapsed for less. What can you do? Kill her? Kill him? Kill both? Risky choice, all three. Kill yourself? Not quite to the point. Here are a number of possible solutions to your problem. If they fail, remember: You have eight more tries. Where preppiness is concerned, you *can* go home again.

1. Make him wear a cat mask. Not much good if he's got a lot of malamute, dachshund, or saluki in him.

2. Make her wear a dog mask. It's a tough thing to ask of your own fur and blood, but she's got your image to think of, doesn't she?

3. The black sheep approach: Every family's got one, even the noblest. Make it a joke and hope your sister's beau is housebroken.

"Doctor, I have terrible dreams about castration."

At his psychiatrist.

THE PRISTINE
CHAPEL

WEDDING BELLE

WEDDING PRESENTS

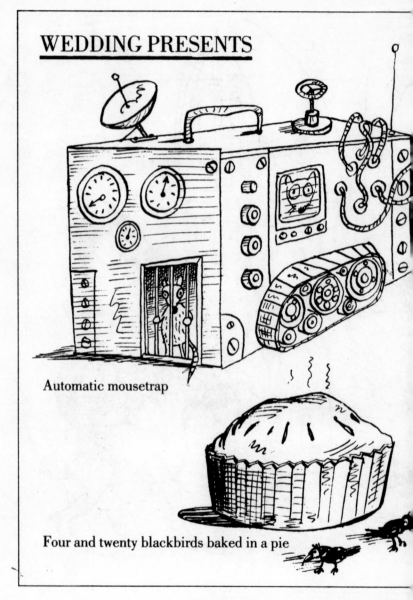

Automatic mousetrap

Four and twenty blackbirds baked in a pie

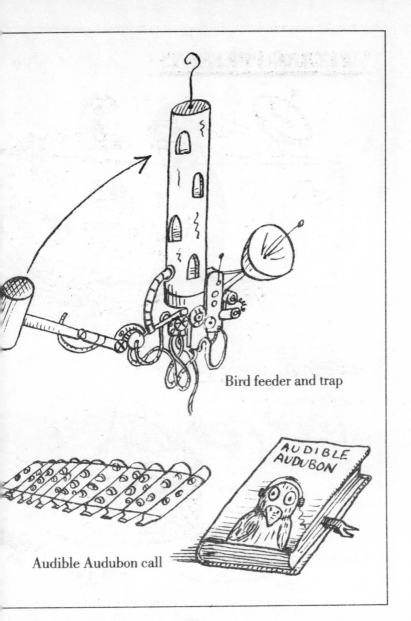

Bird feeder and trap

Audible Audubon call

AUDIBLE AUDUBON

WEDDING PRESENTS

Edible decoy

Mouse server

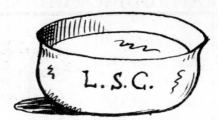

Sterling water dish (monogrammed)

Catnip-filled Snoopy

Potholder

MATERNITY WARD

L. Stanford Cat XVIII
L. Stanford Cat XVIX
L. Stanford Cat XX
L. Stanford Cat XXI
L. Stanford Cat XXII
L. Stanford Cat XXIII
L. Stanford Cat XXIV
L. Stanford Cat XXV
L. Stanford Cat XXVI

HOBBIES & PURSUITS

Catapulting

Caterwauling

Catfish

Catalogs

HOBBIES & PURSUITS

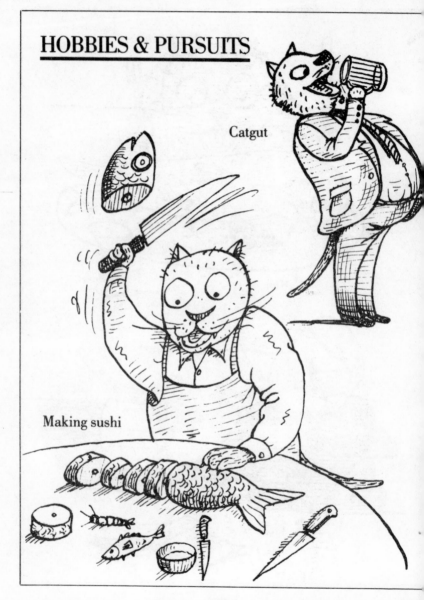

Catgut

Making sushi

Categorizing

Caterpillars